Make in a Day

WEDDING CRAFTS

Natalie Wright

Dover Publications, Inc.
Mineola, New York

To my husband, Dallan, who graciously helped with my own DIY wedding 22 years ago, and has been by my side helping with DIY projects ever since.

A very special thanks to Darice® Craft Supplies with whom I have partnered for many crafty adventures over the years. They have graciously donated many of the supplies in this book so that I may showcase how easily you really can DIY your own wedding.

Bibliographical Note

Make in a Day: Wedding Crafts is a new work, first published by Dover Publications, Inc., in 2019.

International Standard Book Number

ISBN-13: 978-0-486-82216-7
ISBN-10: 0-486-82216-8

Manufactured in the United States by LSC Communications
82216802   2019
www.doverpublications.com

CONTENTS

When I was young, my mother started a business at home as an event planner. She was my first introduction to DIY weddings! Instead of just hiring out different companies to oversee the food and flowers, she often spent long nights at home prepping supplies and creating everything herself to save on costs. She quickly became the most popular wedding planner in our neighborhood, and my first job as a young teen was working long hours on the weekend beside her. I spent many late hours serving wedding guests and cleaning up after each event.

Not only did my mother teach me how to prep for a big party or event, but she also taught me the importance of making things myself. As a young child, I loved seeing her confidence grow as the wedding guests complimented her aesthetics and creativity. Saving the wedding couple money was certainly a big hit too! A lot of the inspiration for the projects in this book comes from those deep-rooted lessons from my mother. Create it yourself, or do without.

Now, as a mother with a big family of my own, I use those same principles and lessons in my own home. Whether it's helping a friend throw a big event or just decorating my own little home in Kentucky, I love finding ways to be creative and thrifty with my home decor.

When I am not helping a friend with a party or wedding, I share my creative endeavors on my personal blog, www.natalme.com. I love to upcycle items, which you will see from the projects in this book.

To keep an eye on all of my creative adventures (and failures!), be sure to follow me on Instagram at @natalme.

Natalie

Place Cards

The wonderful thing about using elements from nature is that they are often free! With all of the many expenses involved in a wedding, it's nice to have a little handmade decor that looks great and doesn't cost a lot. For this project, try a variety of leaves and elements from nature to get the look you want. Be sure to dry your leaves by pressing them in between paper towels in a heavy book for two to three weeks before using them.

To make this project, you will need:

* Dried leaves
* Gold craft paint
* Permanent marker
* Paintbrush
* Wood slice place card holder
* Gold-painted cardstock and double-stick tape (optional)

1 Gather your supplies. Most craft paints work well on leaves, but you may wish to test your paint on a leaf before you begin.

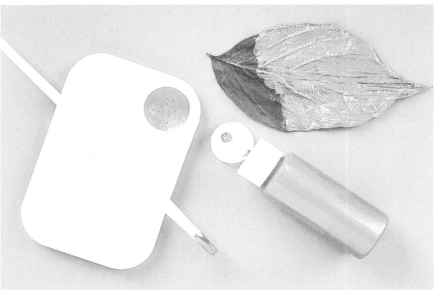

2 To get started, make sure your leaves are completely dry. Using your paintbrush, paint one side of each leaf and let it dry. Flip it over and paint the back. For thin or brittle leaves, use a soft paintbrush and paint with light brushstrokes.

3 Once dry, paint a second coat on your leaves, front and back. Let them dry completely. If your leaves need a little extra stability, add some matching cardstock to the backs with double-stick tape.

4 Using a permanent pen or marker, personalize each leaf with the name of a wedding guest. If you are an expert at hand lettering, use a thin, round paintbrush and craft paint to hand paint each name. You can personalize either one side or both sides.

5 Using your craft glue, place a small dab of glue inside your wood slice place card holder. This will give your leaf a little stability and help it stay in place. Gently slide your leaf inside the place card holder and allow the glue to dry.

TIP: Permanent markers come in many widths and colors. Play around to get the look you want; you don't have to use black!

Table Centerpiece

Paint marbling is one of my favorite creative outlets. It is the method of creating patterns on paper, glass, or fabric that look similar to smooth marble stone. By using a marble medium available at most craft stores, you are able to create patterns that literally "float" on top of your original layer, creating one-of-a-kind designs. Before painting your glass jar, practice on scrap paper or wood.

To make this project, you will need:

* Glass mason jar(s)

* Plastic cups and plastic spoon

* 2 oz. craft paint in 3 or 4 colors

* Craft paint marbling medium

* Wax paper or plastic wrap
  (for drying stage)

* Pie tin

* Paper towels and baby wipes
  (for cleanup)

* Apron and latex gloves
  (to protect clothing)

* Painter's tape (optional)

1. Gather your supplies. You may want to have on hand paper towels and baby wipes. I also like to wear an apron and latex gloves to cut down on the mess. Be sure to work in a well-ventilated area and use a craft paint that is nontoxic.

2. To create your marbling paint, first pour 2 ounces of craft paint in at least three colors in individual plastic cups. I highly recommend disposable cups since they can easily be left out to dry, and then reused by peeling off the leftover paint.

3 Compare the amount of paint in each cup to make sure you have the same amount of each color. Using your marbling medium, pour 1–2 tablespoons of medium in each cup. The amount of medium you use will result in the creation of smaller or larger "cells" in your paint. When you use more medium, the cells separate more, creating larger cells.

4 Using a plastic spoon, stir the medium in each cup 2 or 3 times, being careful not to stir too much. You can use the same spoon for each cup if you start with the lightest paint color and move on to the darkest. It's okay if the different paint colors get mixed together a little.

5 Take a clean cup and pour each of your mixed colors inside, layering them one at a time. Try to pour the paint directly into the middle of the cup. Use your spoon one more time to gently stir 2 or 3 times. This will allow the paint to mix together gently but not completely mix the separate colors into one solid color.

6 Place your glass jar on a pie tin and slowly pour your paint on the desired areas. You can pour only on the bottom half of your jar like I did, or cover the jar completely with paint. I prefer a messy look, but you can easily add painter's tape to your jar to create straight lines.

7 Set your jar aside on wax paper or plastic to dry. Use a small paintbrush to add paint to any uncovered areas where the paint didn't run.

8 Repeat the process covering as many glass jars as you need. Mix fresh paint for each jar, otherwise your colors will start to appear "muddy." Work quickly and be careful not to over-stir your paint!

TIP: For fresh flowers, it is best to paint the outside of your jars. If you plan to put dry items inside your jars, such as string lights, you may prefer to paint the inside instead.

Wedding Card Book

When I was little, I loved saving birthday cards from friends and family. My mother would carefully help me wrap them in ribbon and place them inside a keepsake box. It was always fun to go back each year and read the thoughts and notes from the special people in my life. This keepsake book is a fun way to remember those who helped celebrate your big day, and an easy way to reflect back each year on your anniversary.

To make this project, you will need:

* Wedding notes, cards, and gift tags
* Metal rings
* Scissors
* Hole punch
* Pencil, eraser, and ruler
* Baker's twine and ribbons
* Alphabet stickers (optional)

1. Gather your supplies. Metal rings that can easily open or close are often called binder rings or loose-leaf rings. They are available at most office supply stores and online. The size of your rings will depend on how many cards you want to include in your book. I use a 2" ring, but I would recommend a 3" ring if you have a lot of cards and want to include notes and gift tags.

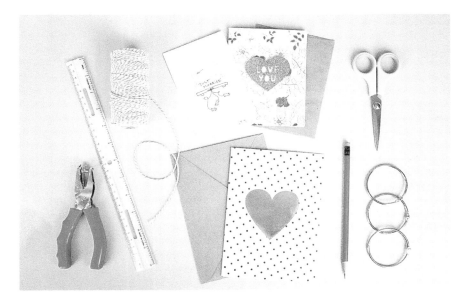

2. To get started, select one of your larger-sized cards, and determine the spacing you want to have between each punched hole. I would recommend spacing your holes at least 2" apart. After determining your distance, use a pencil to lightly mark on the front of your card where your holes should go.

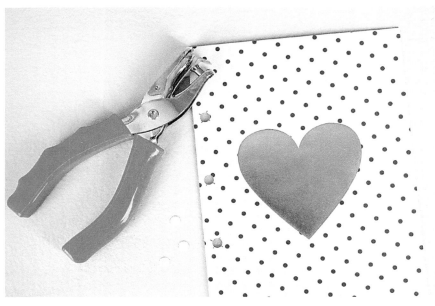

3 Using your hole punch tool, punch holes where you marked your measurements. Use your eraser to gently erase any remaining pencil marks. You will then use this first card as a guide for the rest of your cards and keepsakes.

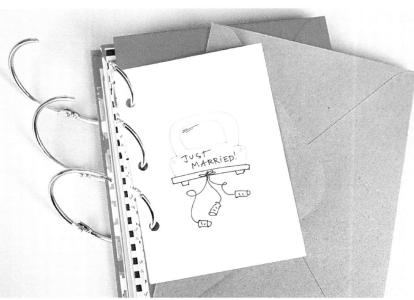

4 Punch the remainder of your cards and notes, assembling them together on your binder rings. It may be helpful to insert the cards one at a time to keep them aligned in all three rings.

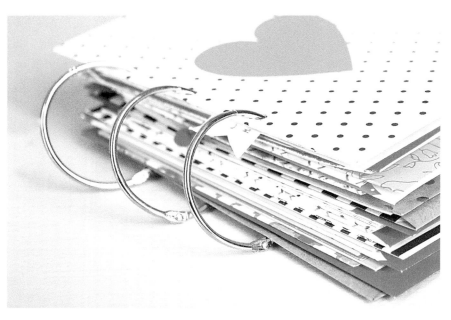

5 Insert the remainder of your cards, and close the rings snugly. Be sure to place a favorite card or keepsake on the top. The great thing about binder rings is they can easily be reopened if you want to add more cards later on.

6 Gather baker's twine and ribbons to embellish your book. You can purchase new ribbons or use any that you might have received with your gifts and cards.

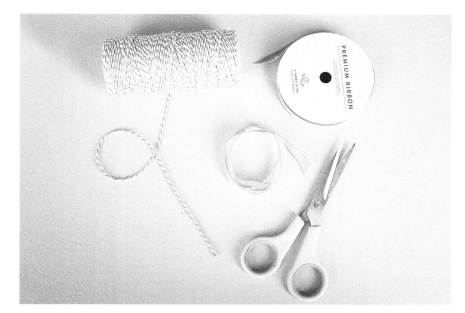

7 Using your scissors, cut your ribbons and twine in 4" strips. Wrap them around your rings and tie a double knot, allowing them to hang outside your card assortment. Trim wider ribbons at an angle to help prevent fraying.

8 Use stickers or hand lettering to personalize the top of your book. You can also include your names, wedding date, or a favorite quote!

TIP: If you love the envelopes that came with your cards, include them in your book! Envelopes make great pockets for the smaller gift tags or gift receipts that you want to save.

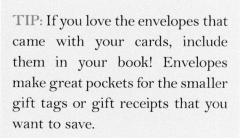

Photo Display

Vintage wood hangers are a great object for creating a unique display. My mother started collecting these years ago for storing her pressed sheets and elegant tablecloths. I was thrilled when she gave me several for creating this fun project. You can easily find them online or in antique stores, and they are often priced at just a dollar or two. Look for ones that show some distressing in the wood but have clean functional hardware on top so that they still are able to open and close.

To make this project, you will need:

* Watercolor paper

* Craft paint (matte)

* Vintage wood pants hanger(s)

* Adhesive

* Printed wedding or other photo(s)

* 1" flat paintbrush

* Ruler and pencil (optional)

1. Gather your supplies. A heavyweight, textured watercolor paper measuring about 9" x 12" would work best for this project. Your photos can be printed any size. My photos are 8" x 10" and printed on a heavyweight paper with a matte finish.

2. Trim your watercolor paper to the desired size. I left my paper at 9" x 12", but you may want to trim it down depending on the size of your wood hanger. Next, using your matte craft paint and your 1" flat paintbrush, loosely paint a rectangle on your paper leaving about ½" unpainted on the sides.

3 Use long, flat brushstrokes to apply your paint evenly. Feel free to cover the entire surface or leave some white areas exposed.

4 Allow the matte paint to fully dry, then add a second coat if needed. Matte paint tends to dry quickly and has a soft, silky feel.

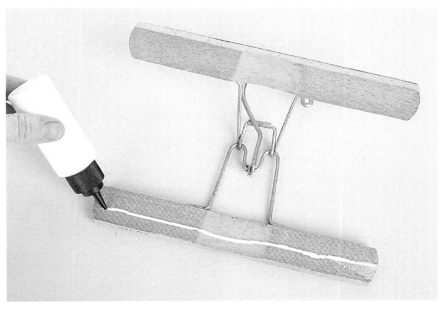

5 While your painted watercolor paper dries, clean off your wood hanger using a mild soap and water. Let it dry completely. Use a safe, water-based archival adhesive to place a long strip of glue on the inside of your wood hanger. Be sure to cover the entire length of the wood.

6 Gently place your watercolor paper inside your wood hanger, aligning the top of the paper with the top of the wood. Gently press down on the paper with your fingers, making sure the glue makes contact with the paper.

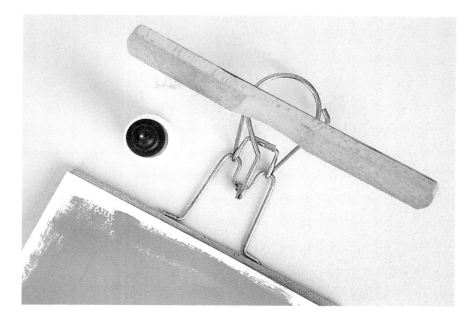

7 Repeat the glue process by placing a long line of glue on top of your paper where the wood hanger will come down on it. Close your hanger to create a tight seal. Wait 2–3 hours to let the glue fully dry.

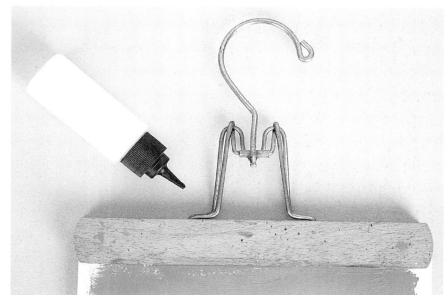

8 Using the same glue or a double-sided, archival-safe tape, adhere your printed photo to the top of your watercolor paper. You can estimate where it goes, or use a ruler and pencil to measure the sides and top evenly before adhering the photo.

TIP: Create variety with wood hangers of different sizes or by painting your watercolor paper in assorted colors.

Guest Gift

It has become more and more customary to show your appreciation to wedding guest attendees by giving them a small gift when they attend your reception. Guests do not come with big expectations; in this case it really is the thought that counts. Contemporary weddings are gifting everything from office supplies monogrammed with the couple's initials to candy buffets with take-home treat bags. I always think it's nice to give something organic that represents new life and longevity. A small houseplant is a wonderful way to represent that a good marriage requires a little nourishment and love each day. Pair a houseplant with a whimsical berry basket, and your wedding gift is sure to be loved for many months after the reception.

To make this project, you will need:

* Wood berry basket(s)
* Hot glue gun and glue sticks
* Paper doilies
* Gold craft paint
* Mini clothespins

* Jute or twine
* ½" flat paintbrush
* Scissors
* Succulent or small houseplant(s)
* Kraft paper sticker label(s)

1. Gather your supplies. Berry baskets come in wood or papier-mâché–like materials and are easy to purchase in bulk online. They often can be found in a variety of colors, so they are easy to match with your wedding decor.

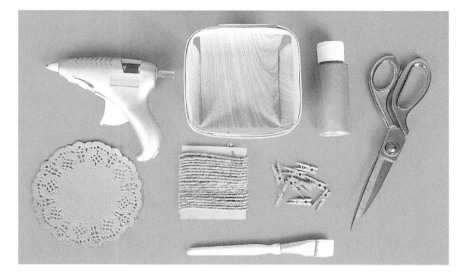

2. To get started, use your gold craft paint and ½" flat paint brush to add some color and shine to the top portion of your basket. Be sure to customize your color to match your wedding theme. Let dry completely, then add a second coat of paint if needed.

3 While your paint dries, prep your doilies by folding them in half, then cutting along the fold making two pieces.

4 Use your hot glue gun to adhere a doily to each basket with the cut line at the bottom. Doilies are delicate, so be sure to use only as much glue as you need.

5. Wrap jute or twine around your basket and tie with a bow. Write a simple thank you note on the kraft label, and attach it to your gift basket with a mini clothespin.

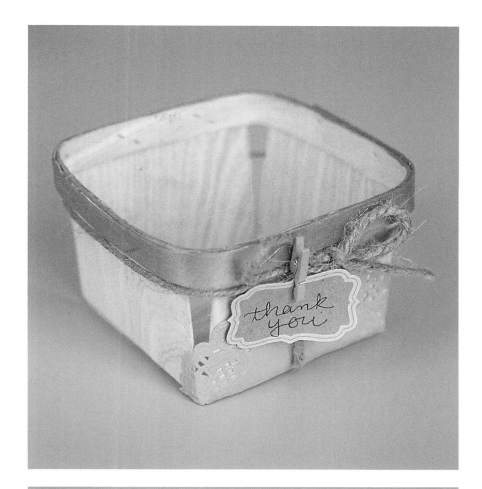

6. Keeping the houseplant or succulent in its original container (without drainage holes), insert it into your decorated basket. Be sure to check the soil to make sure it isn't too dry. You may wish to wait until the day before your wedding to finish this last step.

TIP: Succulents and cacti are great plants to gift as they can go several days or weeks without being watered. The last thing you want to worry about the day before your wedding is dry houseplants!

Silverware Holder

Whether your wedding reception food is a formal affair or laid-back buffet style, showcasing your silverware in a fun way can really enhance your wedding theme and colors. By painting simple designs with watercolor paints, you can create lovely custom place settings that are sure to wow your guests. No art degree is needed when it comes to painting simple flowers, ombré color schemes, or delicate greenery. You can find inexpensive watercolor paints and paper pads at most craft stores. This is a really fun project to make before the wedding with your bridesmaids.

To make this project, you will need:

* Watercolor paper

* Watercolor paints

* Small paintbrush

* Ruler and pencil

* Metallic washi tape

* Craft glue

* Ribbon or burlap bow(s)

* Scissors

1. Gather your supplies. Watercolor paints can be purchased in a palette or tube. Select the colors that best suit your wedding theme. Smooth or textured watercolor papers are great for this project.

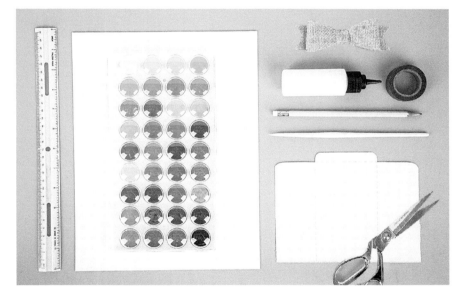

2. Photocopy the provided pattern that appears on the inside back cover of this book. Use scissors to cut it down to size following the line guides on the pattern.

3 Trace the provided pattern onto your watercolor paper. If using a standard size watercolor paper, you should be able to fit two patterns on each sheet.

4 Use your scissors to cut the traced pattern. Be sure to cut the rounded bottom edges evenly.

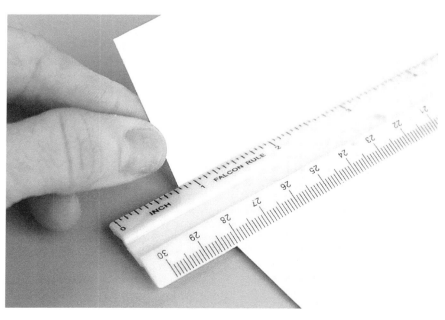

5 Using a ruler, score and fold the bottom tab and two sides. Reopen your silverware pocket.

6 Using your watercolor paints and paintbrush, paint a simple pattern on one side of your cut pattern.

7 Using craft glue, adhere the two sides of the silverware holder together. Let dry completely.

8 Embellish your silverware holder with metallic washi tape, ribbon, burlap, or jute. Insert your silverware and position at your place setting.

TIP: For a buffet-style wedding, place multiple silverware holders inside a fun container at the front of your food table. A ceramic vase, metal bucket, or simple wood box will make a perfect container to hold your whimsical silverware sleeves.

Wedding Confetti

I would much rather have colored confetti thrown at me instead of traditional rice any day! The bright colors and lightweight paper are a fun way to celebrate any festivities, and the individual vellum cones make it really fun to pass out to your guests. You can punch your own confetti with a hole punch, or buy pre-punched confetti in bulk. Be sure to purchase confetti in the colors that best match your wedding theme. You can easily find confetti in metallic hues as well!

To make this project, you will need:

* Paper vellum sheets
* Hot glue gun and glue sticks
* Paper tags made online or by hand

* Mini gold staples and mini stapler
* Scissors
* Paper confetti

1. Gather your supplies. The tags shown here were printed from an online template. You can make your celebration tags the same way; but you can also create your own by hand lettering on either store-bought or hand-cut tags. Paper confetti comes in all shapes and sizes and can be purchased in bulk online.

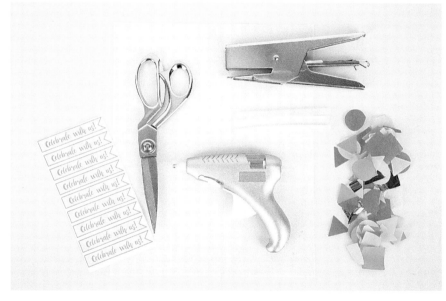

2. To get started, decide how many confetti holders you will need. Each vellum sheet will be folded and cut into four pieces. Vellum is a very delicate material and can easily be torn, so cut carefully along your fold lines. You can also use a paper trimmer for more precise measurements.

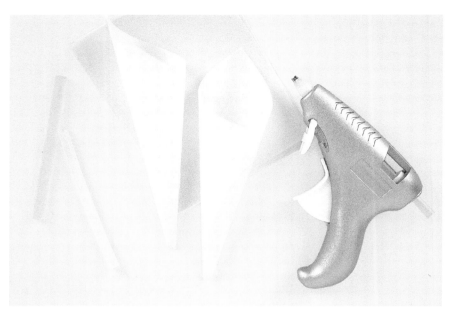

3 Roll your cut vellum pieces into a cone shape. Using your hot glue gun, adhere the outside edge of your vellum cone to seal it together. Let the glue dry completely.

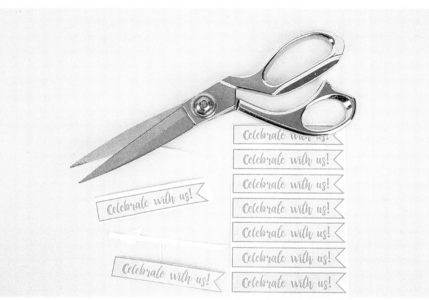

4 Print out the sheet of celebration tags and cut the individual pennants with your scissors. If you have done your celebration tags by hand, make sure you have the correct amount that you will need for your confetti holders.

5 Using a mini stapler, attach the tag to each vellum cone at the top. You can easily customize your own tags with your initials, wedding date, or a favorite quote.

6 Fill your paper cones with confetti to the top. Gently tap the cone to fit as much confetti as you can without squishing it too tightly together.

7 Use a fun container to hold your confetti until it is ready for use. A vintage wood box, metal bucket, or ceramic vase will make great storage options for your confetti cones.

TIP: Invite your guests to throw confetti at the same time, allowing for a great photo opportunity that you will cherish for years to come!

Table Numbers

I have been collecting vintage glass bottles for many years. They are easy to find and affordable to buy, so they are the perfect solution for creating a whimsical display for your table numbers. Since glass containers come in a variety of sizes, consider decorating the outside of the glass with flowers or the inside of the glass with lights for a unique look and feel.

To make this project, you will need:

* Vintage glass bottles
* Wood bases
* 220-grit sandpaper
* ½" flat paintbrush
* Craft glue

* Craft paint
* Metal house numbers
* Epoxy glue (optional)
* Silk flowers or lights (optional)

1. Gather your supplies. Glass bottles are easy to find at local vintage and antique stores. Look for ones that can easily be cleaned and don't have any cracks in case you want to fill yours with fresh flowers. For your house numbers, you can purchase the same style or all different. They can also be painted if you want them to be a different color.

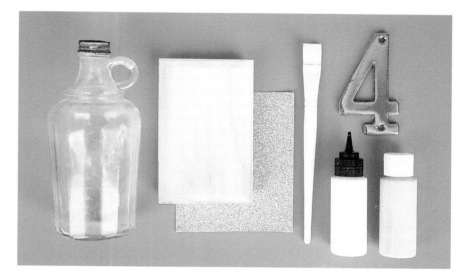

2. Using 220-grit sandpaper, lightly sand each wood base, smoothing any uneven areas. These little decorative wood pieces are found at most craft and hobby stores.

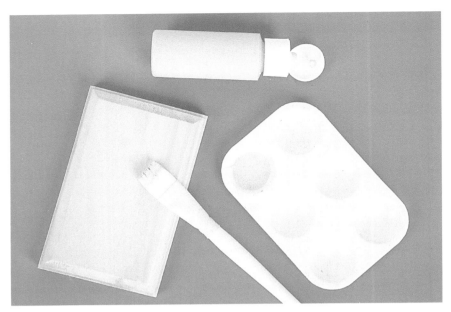

3 Use your craft paint and ½" flat paintbrush to paint your wood base. Let the wood dry completely, then add a second coat if needed. Be sure to use an outdoor, multisurface craft paint if your table numbers will be used outside.

4 Gather the house numbers needed for how many tables you will be setting up at your reception. Paint the numbers if desired. You can also try to find vintage brass house numbers for an eclectic feel.

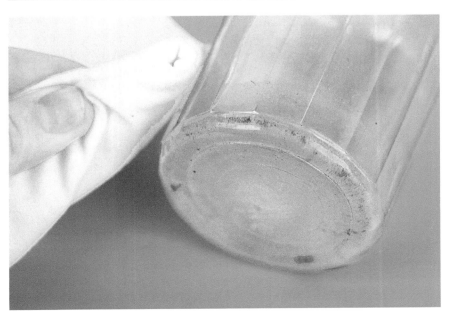

5 While your paint dries, clean your vintage glass bottles using mild soap and water. You will want to clean the insides as well with warm water and a few drops of bleach if you plan to add flowers and water.

6 Using your craft glue, adhere your metal numbers to the outside of the glass bottles. Craft glue will work as a temporary adhesive; however if you want something more permanent, be sure to use an epoxy glue available at most hardware stores.

7 Attach each bottle to a wood base using your craft glue. Let the glue dry completely.

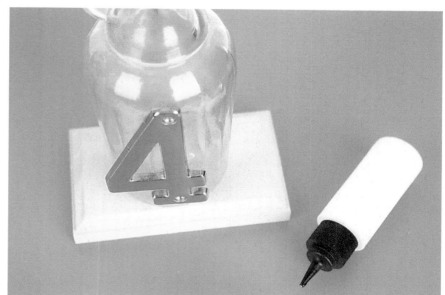

8 Create as many table numbers as you need. Feel free to use different shapes and sizes for the glass bottles and different styles for the numbers.

TIP: Embellish your wood bases with flowers if desired. Silk flowers and leaves can easily be glued to the wood bases and glass bottles to create a festive look.

Star Tablescape

The popularity of upcycling old items at weddings is on the rise, and it's no surprise. Vintage items are often inexpensive to buy and can bring a sense of heartwarming nostalgia to the wedding guests. These vintage folding rulers were common in households in the early 1900s, and they are a fun and creative way to decorate your wedding table. Look for inexpensive folding rulers online, at yard sales, or even try making your own with long pieces of craft wood. When the festivities are over, use your leftover stars to decorate your first home and remind you of your special event.

To make this project, you will need:

* Vintage folding rulers

* Hot glue gun and glue sticks

* ½" flat paintbrush

* Water-based wood varnish, matte or satin

* Clean dry cloth and mild soap

1. Gather your supplies. Be sure to find a water-based varnish with a matte or satin finish and work in a well-ventilated area. For your glue, a low-temperature glue gun will work great and allow you to remove the glue without damaging your vintage rulers.

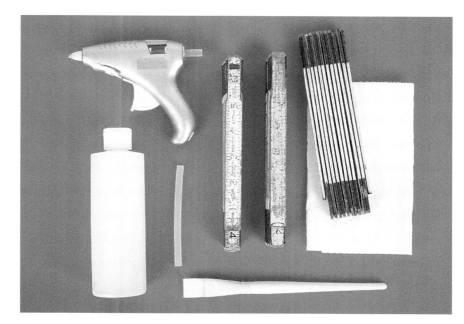

2. To get started, first use the dry cloth and mild soap to clean your ruler of any dust or dirt. Vintage rulers often have rusty hinges based on where they have been used or stored, so you may need to do some heavy cleaning before you get started. If hinges are stuck and you need to position them, a little sewing machine lubricant will do the trick.

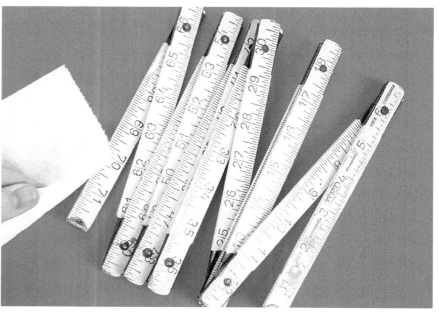

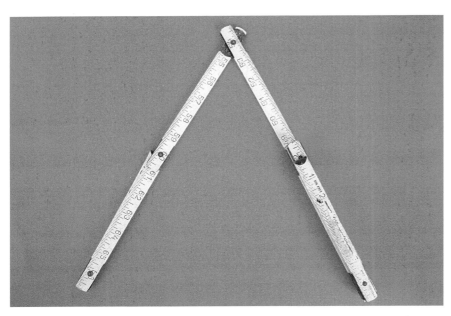

3 To fold your ruler in the shape of a large star, open your ruler into a triangle top, folding two sections at a time.

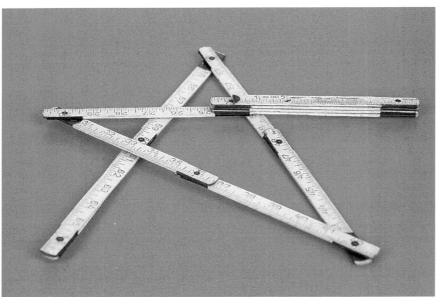

4 Lay your ruler down flat and fold two more sections, continuing in a star pattern. Be gentle while folding as the hinges may be delicate.

5 Finish folding the remainder of your star. Vintage folding rulers typically have twelve pieces attached with eleven hinges. It only takes ten pieces to create a large star. You can fold the excess pieces to keep the entire ruler intact, or carefully remove the extra pieces to create additional stars.

6 Use a low-temperature glue gun to add a pea-sized amount of glue to close the star, sealing it together. You can add small dabs of glue to the cross sections to add additional stability if needed.

7 Repeat the steps to create enough stars for a tablescape. To make a small star, you only need to fold five sections instead of ten. Let the glue completely cool and set before going on to the next step.

8 Using your ½" flat paintbrush and water-based varnish, give the rulers a good coating of sealant. Let your varnish completely dry and cure before use.

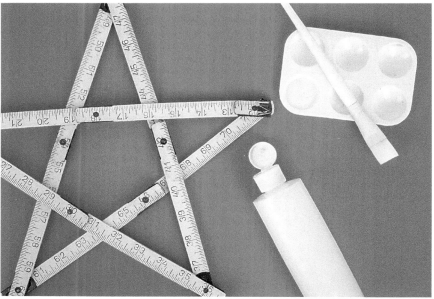

TIP: If your vintage rulers are in really bad shape, consider painting them with a vintage-inspired color. You can also create folding rulers from scratch with thin balsa wood and craft glue found at most craft stores.

Keepsake Tags Display

A display made specially for the messages from your guests is a great DIY project for a wedding as it can easily be used in your home afterward. By upcycling a few wood spindles, you can quickly create a fun way for wedding guests to share their love through simple paper tags. Display the sweet notes after the wedding, and update it with favorite letters and correspondence as time goes on.

- 4 new or vintage wood spindles
- Wood clothespins
- Craft paint in 2 or 3 colors
- Twine and scissors
- Paper tags

- Washi tape in assorted colors and patterns
- ½" flat paintbrush
- Wood or craft glue
- Electric saw or hand saw
- 100-grit sandpaper (if needed)

1. Gather your supplies. You can purchase and paint new wood spindles from your local hardware store or find vintage ones like I did. Wood spindles are used on chair backs, baby cribs, and even as balusters going up a staircase. Determine the right shape and size for your project before you begin.

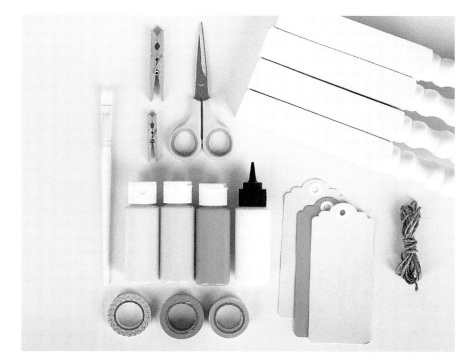

2. To get started, use an electric saw or hand saw to cut a diagonal line at the end of each spindle, measuring four inches from the bottom.

3 Use sandpaper to smooth the cut edges of each spindle, if needed.

4 Line two spindles together at the ends, creating a right angle. Using your wood glue, add a dime-sized amount of glue to the ends of each spindle, and adhere them together. Allow glue to dry completely. Repeat until you have created a square.

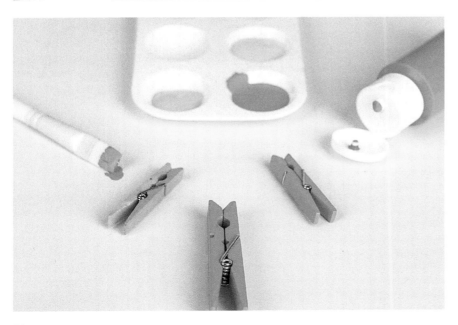

5 While the glue dries, choose your first paint color and paint your wood clothespins. You may wish to carefully disassemble each clothespin so no paint gets on the hinges.

6. Repeat the process by painting additional colors on your remaining clothespins. Add a second coat of paint if needed. Allow your clothespins to dry completely.

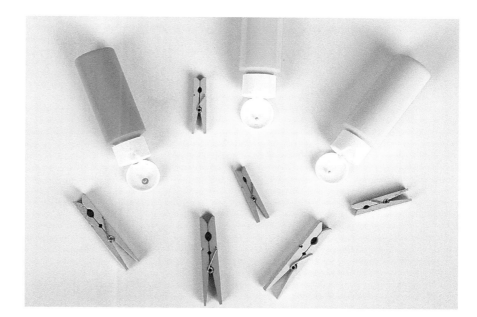

7. Purchase or pre-cut paper tags for the messages. Determine which of your washi tape patterns will be placed on which color tag. Try rotating designs for an eclectic look. You may wish to write a note on one or two to encourage your guests to "sign in" and leave a note for the wedding couple.

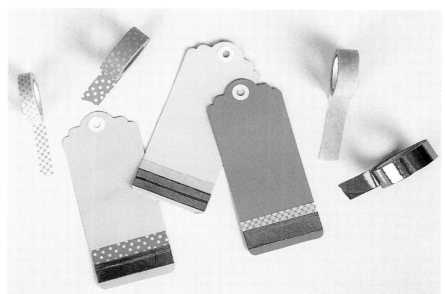

8. When the spindles are dry, wrap twine around them, from the top to the bottom, creating a new layer every 2–3 inches (refer to the finished photo). Tie a double knot at the bottom. Hang the blank tags on the frame or place them in a pretty container until the guest messages are written.

TIP: The wedding couple can also remove the tags and place them on a metal ring to flip through and remember their special day.

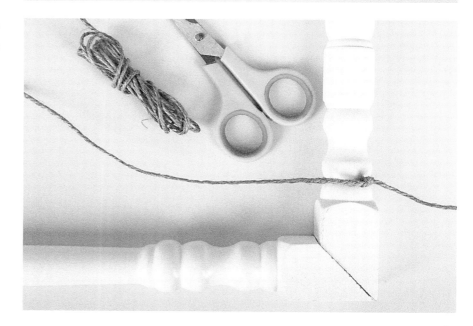
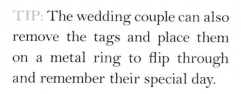

Glitter Sneakers

It just doesn't feel like a wedding without a little sparkly glitter! I will take a pair of comfortable glitter sneakers over high heels any day. These DIY sneakers are surprisingly durable and easy to make. Whether a single pair is being made just for the bride or the bride is crafting glitter sneakers with her bridesmaids, this fun project is sure to bring some wedding prep bliss.

To make this project, you will need:

* White canvas sneakers
* Pink chunky glass glitter
* ½" flat paintbrush
* Craft glue or decoupage glue
* Paper towels to protect surfaces

1 Gather your supplies. Fine glitter or glass glitter can be used in this project, but I prefer chunkier glass glitter as it seems to have better coverage and doesn't shed as much as traditional glitter. Feel free to use multiple colors of glitter for an ombré effect.

2 To get started, first remove the shoelaces from your sneakers. You will also want to determine how much glitter you want to use to cover your sneakers. I love the two-tone look that I went with, but you can easily cover the entire pair.

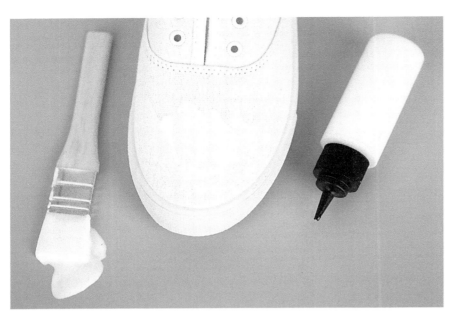

3 Next, using your flat paintbrush, coat your shoes with a generous amount of craft glue or decoupage glue. Try to put a thick, even coat on the entire area you wish to cover with glitter.

4 While the glue is still wet, sprinkle a thick coat of glitter over the glued area of the shoe. Use your brush to add glitter to any missing areas with gentle dabs of glue and glitter. This process can definitely get messy, so embrace the glitter and have fun!

5 Allow the glue and glitter to fully dry, about 2–3 hours. Go back and touch up any areas needed with additional glue and glitter.

6 When you are happy with your glitter coverage, use a clean brush to add another coat of clear glue to the entire top surface of your shoes. This will help seal in the glitter underneath and will help minimize any glitter falling off as you walk.

7 When the glue is completely dry and cured, replace the laces on your shoes being careful not to disturb the glitter areas.

TIP: To add more pizzazz to your shoes, consider changing out the traditional laces with lace trim or a fun ribbon!

Lighting Decor

Glass tea light holders are an essential part of wedding decor, and these fun, mercury glass containers can be used in a variety of ways. Whether using battery-operated tea lights or flowers, this unique lighting display is an inexpensive way to create some fun wedding decor.

To make this project, you will need:

* 1" x 6' wood board and chop saw
* Glass tea light holders
* Hammer and 1" nails
* 220-grit sandpaper
* Wood or craft glue

* Matte craft paint and flat paintbrush
* Ruler, pencil, and twine
* Electric drill and ½" drill bit
* Right angle (optional)

1. Gather your supplies. You will need one 6' board for each tea light decor piece that you want to make. This photo shows a sample of the wood already cut into the sizes you will need.

2. Cut your 1" x 6' wood board into four pieces, two measuring 16" and two measuring 20". Use your 220-grit sandpaper to sand and smooth any rough areas on all four of your wood boards.

3 Place your wood boards on a flat surface creating a box shape. Use a right angle if needed to make sure your corners are evenly aligned. Gently dab each corner with glue and press firmly together.

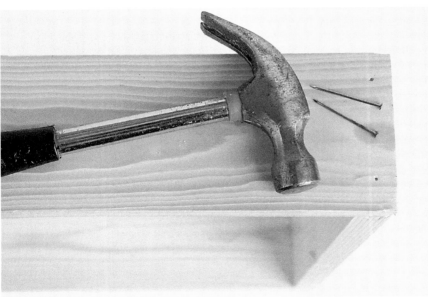

4 Using your 1" nails and hammer, lightly hammer two nails in each corner while your glue is still wet. Allow your glue to fully dry. Reinforce with additional nails if needed.

5 Place your wood box upright. Using a ruler and pencil, measure the placement for your twine to hang your tea light holders. I evenly spaced five holes on mine, but you can add as many as you can fit.

6 Using an electric drill and ½" drill bit, drill holes in your marked areas. Carefully remove any wood shavings. Use your sandpaper to gently smooth any rough areas around your drilled holes.

7 Paint your wood box using your matte craft paint and a flat paintbrush. Be sure to choose a color that coordinates with your wedding decor. Once your paint is dry, add a second coat if needed. For a distressed look, sand over the corners and edges with your sandpaper.

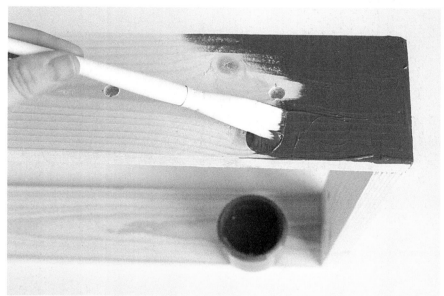

8 Use the twine to attach the tea light holders to your frame. Cut four long twine pieces that measure the same length. Pull each piece through a drilled hole and knot at the top and bottom. Add a small dab of glue to the bottom of your tea lights for added stability if needed.

TIP: Use battery-operated tea lights, string lights, or fairy lights to decorate and light up your decor. Do not use actual candles.

Floral Embroidery Hoop

Crepe paper is one of my most favorite materials to work with. It is very inexpensive to buy and now comes in a wide variety of lovely colors. It is very easy to cut and shape, and most glues work really well with it. I love that with just a small piece of crepe paper I can create flower petals with a lot of depth and dimension. A little bit of this flexible paper really goes a long way.

To make this project, you will need:

* 9" wood embroidery hoop
* Hot glue gun and glue sticks
* Scissors
* Crepe paper in black, green, white, and peach (or colors of your choice)

1 Gather your supplies. Crepe paper comes in inexpensive dollar packs online, but I would suggest spending a little more and getting the higher-quality, thicker crepe paper for just a dollar or two more. You can easily find crepe paper in the perfect colors to match your wedding decor.

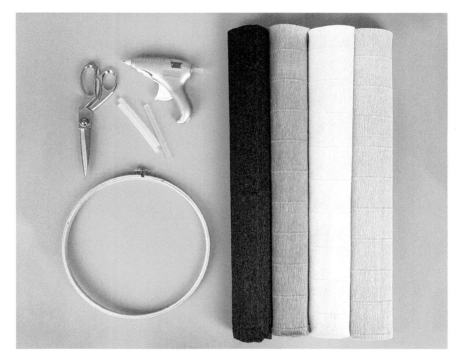

2 Start with cutting your flower petals. For the small flower, with the peach crepe paper, cut 6–8 large oval petals about 4" in height. Cut an additional 4–6 petals about 3" in height. Cut a slit at the bottom of each petal. For the two large flowers, use your white crepe paper to cut 6–8 large oval petals about 6" in height and the additional petals about 5" in height.

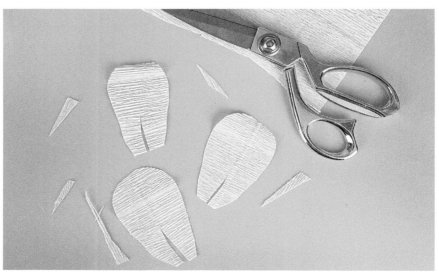

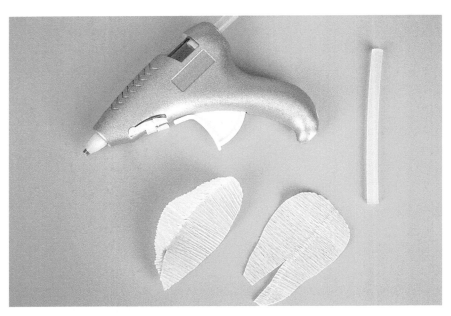

3 Using your glue gun, fold and adhere the bottom of each petal to give it some depth and dimension. Crepe paper can be thin, so use a low-temperature glue gun if you are worried about your adhesive getting too hot.

4 Using your scissors and green crepe paper, cut 4–5 leaves for each flower, measuring from 4" to 6" tall. Fold the leaves in half lengthwise, then reopen them back up.

5 For your flower centers, cut a 2" x 12" strip of black crepe paper. Fold it in half, then fringe cut the open side. Try to cut your slits every ⅛" or smaller, depending on how much fringe you want to have.

6　Holding your cut fringe firmly in place, gently roll one side toward the center. Add a dab of glue as you go. When finished, glue the end piece down and gently tussle the fringe with your fingers.

7　Starting with the small flower, layer your flower petals with the larger petals in the back and the smaller petals on top. Adhere your flower center to the middle. Let your glue cool completely. Repeat for your larger flowers, following the same process to assemble.

8　Add your green leaves to the outside of the flowers. Glue the flowers to the embroidery hoop so that you conceal the screw, adding more green leaves as needed. Create one for each of your bridesmaids.

TIP: If you plan on creating embroidery hoop flowers for your flower girls, attach a small basket to the backside. Cut additional petals and leaves for them to toss as they walk down the aisle.

Marquee Letters Sign

Marquee letters are all the rage at weddings these days, so why not do something unique and fill them with some organic materials? Flowers, pebbles, or moss are all great options for helping your letters stand out. Pick up some inexpensive marquee letters to start, or make your own with an online tutorial!

To make this project, you will need:

* Plastic or metal marquee letters with batteries

* Hot glue gun and glue sticks

* Brick paneling or Masonite™ board

* Ruler or measuring tape

* Green moss

* Old picture frame

* Circular saw

* Screwdriver and wood screws

* Wood glue

1. Gather your supplies. You will want to first determine what you want your letters to spell out, then find the coordinating marquee letters for that phrase. You can make your sign as small or as big as you like! Pick a favorite phrase that means something special for you and your loved one so you can hang it in your home after your special day.

2. To get started, remove your green moss from the package and allow it to air-dry for 2–3 hours. Moss is a living plant and is often packaged while it is still slightly damp. It can have a damp smell, so you may wish to work outdoors or in an open area with good ventilation. Begin by placing your moss inside your marquee to get an idea of how full you want it.

3 Using your hot glue gun, carefully lift up the moss in small sections, apply glue to the marquee letter, and gently place the moss back down. Be sure to use a low-temperature glue gun as the moss is porous and you don't want to burn your skin.

4 Once your glue is dry, lift your marquee letter upside down and gently tap it. Turn it back over and see if there are any areas that also need to be filled. Repeat this process on all of your marquee letters until they are all glued and dry.

TIP: Marquee letters typically come with wired lights and round bulbs, but the bulbs and wiring can easily be removed if you wish to just embellish traditional letters. You can also remove the traditional lights and change them out for colored holiday lights that fit your wedding theme.

5 Using an upcycled frame and brick paneling, measure and cut a backing for your message. Carefully use a circular saw to cut your paneling to size; paint your brick paneling with white house paint, if desired. Let it dry completely before placing in your frame. Adhere the paneling to the frame using wood glue. Allow to dry.

6 Use your measuring tape to make sure your letters will be properly aligned, then attach small screws to hang the letters of your message on the frame. You can add additional cut paper lettering like I did, or spell your entire phrase with marquee lettering. If desired, embellish your frame with felt flowers found in any craft store.

7 Hang your marquee sign in the desired location. Be sure to place new batteries in each letter and turn on before hanging on the previously attached screws. Light-up marquee letters typically illuminate for several hours, but you may wish to have extra batteries on hand just in case.

Wood Lantern

I always like creating something for a party that I can use to decorate my home afterward. Wood lanterns create such a nice ambience for a wedding, but look great on your front doorstep too! You can customize the size of your lantern so it will fit in with your front or back porch decor after your festivities. You can even create two different-sized lanterns that will look great with outdoor candles, fresh flowers, and potted plants placed right inside.

To make this project, you will need:

* 2' x 2' wood

* 1' x 4' wood

* 1' x 2' wood (often called furring strip)

* Charcoal gray craft paint

* White craft paint

* 1" flat paintbrush

* 120-grit and 220-grit sandpaper

* Miter saw or chop saw

* Nail gun or hammer and 2" finishing nails

* Craft or wood glue

1. Gather your supplies.* This is a great project for wood scraps as the size of the lantern can easily be adjusted to work with wood sizes you already have at home. Be sure to use outdoor multisurface craft paint if you plan to keep your lantern outdoors.

   *Not all supplies are shown in this photo. Refer to photos accompanying subsequent steps.

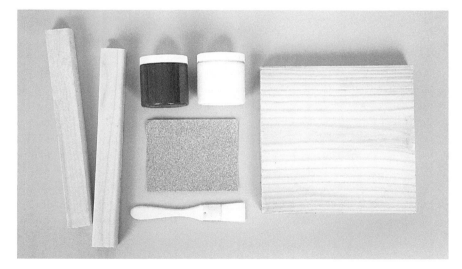

2. Using a chop saw or miter saw, cut your wood pieces to the following dimensions. (For the small lantern, substitute the four 13" pieces for four 9" pieces.)

   Large Lantern:
   4   2" x 2" x 13" pieces
   4   2" x 2" x 1.5" pieces
   2   1" x 8" x 8" pieces
   8   1" x 2" x 5" pieces
   4   1" x 2" x 4" pieces

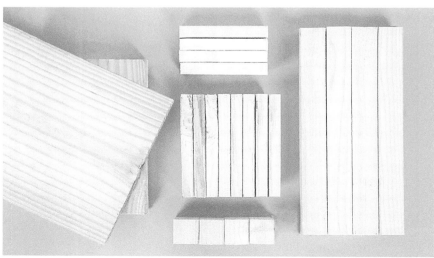

3 Using your 120-grit sandpaper, sand down any rough cuts on your lantern pieces of wood.

4 Wipe away any dirt or dust. Use your finer 220-grit sandpaper to go over the corners and any remaining rough areas on your wood pieces.

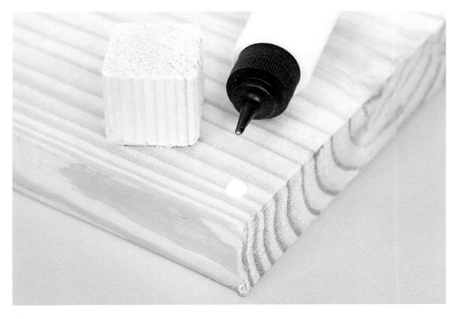

5 Using a water-based craft or wood glue, adhere the four 2" x 2" x 1.5" feet to your 1" x 8" x 8" lantern base. Just a dab of glue will work great. Let your lantern feet dry for 1–2 hours.

6 Using a nail gun or a hammer and 2" finishing nails, attach your feet to the lantern base to give it extra stability.

7 Turn your lantern right side up, and assemble the remaining side pieces working your way from the bottom to the top. Assemble the frame first using the four 2" x 2" x 13" pieces, followed by the 5" side pieces. Be sure to use both glue and nails to assemble your lantern.

8 Assemble the top "lid" piece by using the remaining 1" x 8" x 8" piece of wood and adhering the 4" furring strips creating a square on top. Glue pieces in place. Allow the glue in your entire lantern to dry 2–3 hours. You will also want to lightly sand any areas that are still rough.

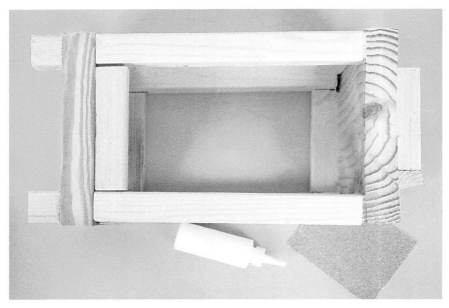

9 Lay your lantern on its side and reinforce with nails where needed. Sand any additional areas that still feel rough to the touch. Wipe away any dust when done with a clean dry cloth.

10 Using your outdoor charcoal gray craft paint, brush the entire inside and outside of your lantern with 1–2 coats. Let the paint dry in between each coat of paint. If your lantern is going outside, turn the lantern over and paint the bottom as well to protect it from moisture.

11 Using your white outdoor craft paint, dry brush a light coat of paint over the entire lantern to give it a contrasting distressed feel. Let it dry completely. Insert flameless battery-operated candles and greenery.

TIP: You don't have to use your oversized candles as a lighting source! Place a clear glass hurricane inside the lantern and fill with flowers, pinecones, or fruit.